Galway GAA in Old Photographs

Jack Mahon

GILL & MACMILLAN

Gill & Macmillan Ltd
Hume Avenue
Park West
Dublin 12
with associated companies throughout the world
www.gillmacmillan.ie

© 2002 Jack Mahon
0 7171 3391 5
Design and print origination by O'K Graphic Design, Dublin
Printed in Malaysia

The paper used in this book is made from the wood pulp of managed forests.
For every tree felled, at least one tree is planted, thereby renewing natural resources.

A catalogue record is available for this book from the British Library.

1 3 5 4 2

Contents

INTRODUCTION   V

GALWAY GAA IN OLD PHOTOGRAPHS   1

Introduction

Hurling in Galway is almost as old as the hills. The game flourished in the stonewall area of South Galway long before the GAA itself was founded in Thurles in 1884. The Statutes of Galway in 1527 banned 'hurling of the little ball with hockey sticks or staves'. In 1791, a young Frenchman named Coquebert de Montbret in his travels visited County Galway, and observed and wrote about hurling there. A hurling game was played in Meelick in 1798. There are numerous other references. Football of a sort was played in Galway as elsewhere long before Michael Cusack formulated rules to govern it. The same Statutes of Galway of 1527 did not ban 'footballe' as they called it. The rough and tumble game which preceded 1884 was popular in North Galway and tales of battles royal between neighbouring parishes still linger. The ball was often made of leather stuffed with hay or a súgán wound to resemble a ball. They started on Sundays after Mass at some half-way point and went on to dusk, a kind of cross-country football test in which nothing was barred.

Michael Cusack

Michael Cusack was born in Carron, County Clare in 1847, the year Daniel O'Connell died, at the height of the great famine. The famine ruined the spirit of Ireland, wiped out its population and almost killed off their uniquely Irish pastimes. To counter this Cusack issued his clarion call to rouse the nation through its games. When Cusack became a teacher his first appointment was to Lough Cutra National School where he served as Principal from 31 December 1866 to October 1871. He had a big influence on the early development of the GAA in County Galway and invited Dr Duggan, the ageing Bishop of Clonfert, to be its first patron. Dr Duggan, because of his age, declined and suggested the younger Dr Croke, Archbishop of Cashel, instead. Otherwise the GAA would have been founded in Galway, in Loughrea specifically.

First Rules

The first rules of gaelic football included much of the rough and tumble game but these became refined in time. Galway reached the first-ever All-Ireland Senior Hurling final when Meelick lost out to Thurles in the 1887 final. In gaelic football Galway (Tuam Krugers) was the first team from Connacht to reach a final before losing to Tipperary (Clonmel Shamrocks) in the 1900 final (home). It is interesting to note the name Kruger, a general in the Boer War, a war in which Irish-born soldiers mutinied and in which the native Irish supported the Boers. Then as now GAA clubs were very national in outlook and clubs often took the names of O'Connell, Sarsfield, Parnell, Davitt, Davis, Wolfe Tone, Grattan, Emmet, along with their own placename to acknowledge their national identity. Galway had to wait until the 1920s to win their first All-Ireland titles – 1923 in hurling and 1925 in gaelic football – and the men who were the stars of these first successes became folk heroes, men like Leonard McGrath (on both teams), Michael 'Knacker' Walsh (Football), Mick Gill (Hurling), Ignatius Harney (Hurling), Mick Donnellan (Football), Jim Power (Hurling) and Tom Molloy (Football).

The 1930s

The 1930s brought much success in gaelic football to Galway when the organisation became more streamlined everywhere and huge crowds travelled to All-Ireland finals, with more Irish people participating in GAA games and Croke Park being developed into a super stadium. Galway was the first team from the West to bring the Sam Maguire cup across the Shannon. In doing so in 1934 the players wore the colours maroon and white for the first time and the crest which has become so much part of the Galway jersey. Before then Galway had played in blue and gold, and also green and white.

Galway could always produce good hurling teams but they suffered for many years from lack of competition elsewhere in the West. They lost semi-final after semi-final, sometimes by close margins, never contesting a final from 1931 to 1952, 22 years in all. However, in 1953 they beat Kilkenny in the semi-final, with men like Seánie Duggan, Johnny Molloy, Joe Salmon, Josie Gallagher and John Killeen. Despite all the beatings at national level they never gave up the ghost and won the Railway Cup for the first time in 1947, captained by that peerless goalkeeper Seánie Duggan.

The footballers had much more success, winning the All-Ireland in 1938 after two hectic games with Kerry and helping in no small way in Connacht's four

Railway Cup wins in the 1930s (those of 1934, 1936, 1937 and 1938). Galway and Mayo were two of Ireland's top teams then and it was Mick Donnellan who led Connacht in their first-ever Railway Cup victory in 1934. Just as in 1925, men like John Dunne, Brendan Nestor, Mick Connaire, Mick Higgins and Dinny O'Sullivan became household names. My own idol then was the great Bobby Beggs, swarthy and tanned. He was larger than life and a cult hero in Galway. One of the great Galway players of that time, Frank Fox, died in the full prime of manhood. The cup for the Galway Senior Football Championship bears his name.

Progressive development

Cusack, who died in 1906, could never have envisaged the massive creation his clarion call delivered in a vibrant GAA which survived early troubles such as the Parnellite Split, the Rising of 1916 and the Civil War to become such a sophisticated structure so soon. Attracting many participants and huge crowds at games, the progressive official structure leaned largely on county boundaries and love of parish. The creation of new grades helped to cater for all increased participation and before we knew it, there were special third level competitions (Sigerson, Fitzgibbon and Ashbourne Cups). There were college competitions, Provincial Championships, minor and junior grades and the development of club and county grounds all over Ireland mostly named after national or religious figures or former GAA greats. Galway played its part in all the new developments as well as providing one of the GAA's first Presidents, P.J. Kelly of Kilnadeema, who reigned from 1889–1895. Camogie too was always strong in Galway and tales are still told of the late Peg Morris, reputed to be Galway's best ever player.

1940s and 1950s

The 1940s provided Galway with a barren period apart from the Railway Cup (Hurling) success of 1947 and three All-Ireland final defeats for Galway's footballers in 1940, 1941 and 1942 when men like Jarlath Canavan and Joe Duggan failed to win a medal. This was the era of Tom Sullivan of Oughterard who, although he missed a medal, is rated one of Galway's greatest ever. This honour can apply also to Fr Paddy Gantly whose priestly duties curtailed a brilliant hurling career. The 1950s brought greater joy. First the hurlers won the

1951 National League very impressively and travelled to New York with the Meath footballers in the autumn of that year, beating New York in the final proper. Then followed the near miss to Cork in the All-Ireland final of 1953. In between Galway won its first Minor Football All-Ireland, captained by Brian Mahon of Dunmore. Then along came Galway's 1956 All-Ireland Senior Football winning team who beat all before them, captained by Jack Mangan of Tuam and powered by Seán Purcell ('The Master'), Frank Stockwell, Tom Dillon, Mattie McDonagh and Frank Evers. I was privileged to play centre half-back on that team alongside fellow half-backs Jack Kissane and Mick Greally. We duly recorded a National Football League success the following year. At that time the Galway hurlers, through some ludicrous scheme, were granted free passage into the All-Ireland finals of 1955, and 1958, only to suffer heavy defeats by Wexford and Tipperary. Whatever chance Galway had after one game in preparation they had no chance at all being thrown in at the deep end.

The 1960s and 1970s

The 1960s was a wonderful decade for Galway football, producing the three-in-a-row team captained by John Donnellan (1964) and Enda Colleran (1965 and 1966), a smashing Minor All-Ireland football team in 1960, and the famed St Jarlath's College Tuam teams with their many Hogan Cup wins. St Jarlath's College emerged as a great gaelic football nursery, with its counterpart in hurling St Mary's College, Galway. Galway's three-in-a-row team was a gifted footballing side, possibly one of the greatest ever in the game. Leydon, Keenan, Garrett, Reynolds, Newell, Tierney, McDermott, Meade, Geraghty ... Cyril Dunne the sharpshooter, Tyrrell and Cleary. Hurling went through a bad patch with Galway being accepted into Munster and failing miserably. They could not get out fast enough to try afresh. But hope was there in the creation of a vibrant Coiste Iomána and the growth of national awareness of the Vocational School system — a scheme which contributed largely to the resurgence of hurling in Galway. The amount of hurling All-Irelands won by Galway County Vocational Schools as a county or as individual school competitions is incredible.

The 1970s started well in ways. Once again there were three defeats in a row in All-Ireland finals (football) – 1971, 1973 and 1974, when men like Liam O'Neill, Billy Joyce and Michael Rooney played in all three finals but won no medal. The Under-21 grade was now well in vogue since the 1960s and Galway brought off the double success in 1972 with men like Iggy Clarke, P.J. Molloy in hurling and John Tobin and Tom Naughton in football. But Galway hurling was on the move, with a National Hurling League success in 1975 and men such as John Connolly (captain), Seán Silke, Joe McDonagh and P.J. Qualter involved. Then followed All-Ireland losses in 1975 and 1979, both to Kilkenny. But the great days lay ahead.

Modern Times

The 1980s saw Galway hurling at its brilliant best. In 1980 they won their first All-Ireland Senior Hurling Championship title since 1923. Will we ever forget the celebrations and Joe Connolly's great speech *tré Gaeilge*? There were also the Under-21 successes and those wonderful Vocational School boys. Our first-ever Minor Hurling crown came in 1983 under Anthony Cunningham, with two more Senior Hurling crowns in 1987 and 1988 under Cyril Farrell as manager. Conor Hayes was the magnificent captain both years. Winning hurling All-Irelands at all levels almost became commonplace. Perish that thought. There has been no Senior Hurling Championship title since but the big day is not far away again. Four Minor crowns since 1992 all point that way. An ignominious Senior Football Championship final defeat to Dublin in 1983 put Galway football back years, though a fine Minor Football success in 1986 did lend hope.

The success of Galway hurling clubs in the club All-Irelands must be mentioned. Castlegar started it all in 1980 followed by Kiltomer 1992, Sarsfields 1993 and 1994 and Athenry 1997, 2000 and 2001. Gaelic football is tops in Galway once again, beginning with Corofin's 1998 club All-Ireland followed by Galway's 98 All-Ireland triumph, both captained by Ray Silke. Then came the 2001 crown with Gary Fahey as captain, managed by that supreme gentlemen John O'Mahony. It is all so recent but unforgettable: the brilliant forward play of Pádhraic Joyce, Derek Savage and Michael Donnellan; the coolness under pressure of Kevin Walsh; Declan Meehan on the burst; the absolute majesty of Jarlath Fallon in the 1998 final v Kildare; or half-backs Tomás Mannion and Seán de Paor defending superbly.

This Book

This book takes a look back in pictures to Galway's GAA years, not forgetting camogie (we are up there with the best having won a Senior crown in 1994 and many other national crowns). I am grateful to all who supplied photographs: men like Frank Burke (Chairman, Galway County Board), Jarlath Cloonan (Athenry), Phelim Murphy (Secretary, Galway Hurling Board). It was a labour of love and I strove to have every photograph captioned properly – christian as well as surnames. Many people promised to supply photographs but deadlines are deadlines. Finally, thanks to the publishers Gill & Macmillan who have, as always, been so professional and helpful.

Jack Mahon
May, 2002

Galway GAA in Old Photographs

This photograph was supplied by Seán Purcell, Galway's greatest ever player. It is an informal shot taken in Croke Park as the Galway players prepare to take on Tyrone in the 1956 All-Ireland semi-final. Galway won by 0-8 to 0-6. From left: Jack Kissane (5), Tom McHugh being spoken to by John 'Tull' Dunne (secretary), Seán Purcell facing the camera, Gerry Kirwan, Tom 'Pook' Dillon (4), Fr Paddy Mahon (chairman) giving last minute advice to his brother Jack, Seán Keeley (2), and on right Frank Stockwell.

Great Fielding Dual 1972

There is nothing better in gaelic football than to see two top players in the air fielding a high ball. This great shot from a Galway v Roscommon Senior Football Championship replay in Tuam in 1972 (won by Roscommon) shows Billy Joyce (on left) contesting the fetch with his great opponent Dermot Earley (Roscommon). Who won the duel? Your guess is as good as mine!

A happy Galway minor football team after defeating Mayo to win the 1986 Connacht final in Hyde Park, Roscommon. FRONT FROM LEFT: Pádhraic Fallon, John Mitchell (substitute), Brian Silke, Maurice McDonagh, the late John Joyce (*captain*), Tommy Finnerty and Tomás Kilcommins. BACK FROM LEFT: Kevin Walsh, Alan Mulholland, Michael Tarpey, Tomás Mannion, Bosco Walsh, Adrian Brennan, Fergal O'Neill, Francis McWalter, Peter Maher. This team later went on to become All-Ireland champions (Galway's 5th in this grade), defeating Cork in the final by 3-8 to 2-7.

Galway v Wexford 1976 All-Ireland Semi-final Draw in Cork

Action from the drawn epic All-Ireland Senior Hurling semi-final played in Páirc Uí Chaoimh, Cork on 15 August 1976 on a beautifully sunny day. The result was Wexford 5-14 Galway 2-23. (Wexford won the replay).FROM LEFT: Niall McInerney and Joe Clarke cover off Wexford full-forward Tony Doran with Iggy Clarke in the background before a huge shirt-sleeved attendance.

The 1938 All-Ireland Senior Football Champions
FRONT FROM LEFT: Frank Cunniffe, Jackie Flavin, Mick Higgins, John Dunne (captain) Ned Mulholland, Mick Raftery. BACK FROM LEFT: Bobby Beggs, Ralph Griffin, John Burke, Jimmy McGauran, Charlie Connolly, Brendan Nestor, Dinny O'Sullivan, Mick Connaire, Martin Kelly. They beat Kerry in a replay to win the title. The drawn game is reputed to be one of the greatest of all finals. They are all dead now but their memory lives on.

1955 Defeated Galway Senior Hurling All-Ireland Team
This was the team that was beaten by Wexford 3-13 to 2-8. FRONT FROM LEFT: Billy O'Neill, Tommy Boland, Paddy Egan, Joe Salmon, Jimmy Duggan (captain) with mascot Paddy 'Whack' Walsh, Paddy 'Mogan' Duggan, Mickey Burke. BACK FROM LEFT: Tim Sweeney, Bernie Power, Jim Fives, Johnny Burke, Tommy Kelly, Joe Young, Billy Duffy, Johnny Molloy.

Galway's All-Ireland Senior Hurling Champions of 1980
FRONT FROM LEFT: Niall McInerney, Séamus Coen, Jimmy Cooney, Joe Connolly (captain), Sylvie Linnane, P.J. Molloy, Bernie Forde. BACK FROM LEFT: Conor Hayes, Steve Mahon, John Connolly, Michael Connolly, Michael Conneely, Frank Burke, Noel Lane, Seán Silke.

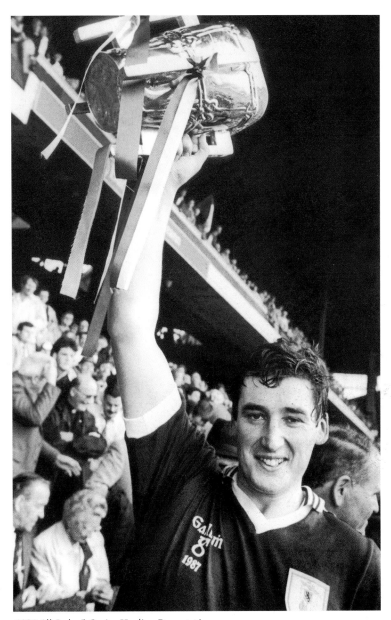

1987 All-Ireland Senior Hurling Presentation
Conor Hayes, captain, raises the Liam McCarthy Cup in triumph after
leading Galway to victory over Kilkenny 1-12 to 0-9. The Kiltomer man
gave great service to club and county over a long career and shares with
Enda Colleran, Jimmy Murray (Roscommon) and Seán Flanagan (Mayo)
the distinction of captaining two All-Ireland successes in a row for men from
the West.

Keeping a Close Eye
Jack Cosgrave, Galway's fine full-back of the 1970s, keeping a very close eye indeed on his opponent Seán O'Neill of Down, as the latter laces his football boot at some stage during the All-Ireland semi-final of 1971 (won by Galway 3-11 to 2-7), while play continued at the other end of the field. Shots like these revive great memories.

Frank Stockwell — Record Breaker

Frank Stockwell is a legend in his native Tuam. Even a road is called after him. In the 1956 football final against Cork he scored a record 2-5 from play — a fantastic achievement in a 60-minute game. Another goal scored by him that day was disallowed. 'Stocky' as he is known in Tuam was years before his time as a forward, his solo-running technique being unique.

Former Colleagues Meet in 1965

This photo was taken at the Player Wills HQ the day after Galway beat Kerry in the All-Ireland final of 1965. In those days receptions for the winning teams took place the Monday after final day. Frank Evers, former team-mate, is present to congratulate Martin Newell and his old midfield partner Mattie McDonagh.

All-Ireland Winning Minor Footballers of 1976
FRONT FROM LEFT: Gay McManus, Pádhraic Conroy, Robert Birmingham, Gerry Burke (captain), Stephen Ruane, Joe Kelly, Ollie Burke. BACK FROM LEFT: Kieran O'Sullivan, Frank Rooney, Barry Brennan, Pádhraic Coyne, Gerry Forde, Ciarán Ó Fatharta, Mattie Coleman, Leo Higgins. This team defeated Cork in the All-Ireland final by 1-10 to 0-6 and was managed by former three-in-a-row All-Ireland goalkeeper (1964–1966) Johnny Geraghty.

Two Midfield Hurling Greats
In 1984, the centenary year of the foundation of the GAA, there were many occasions to honour the heroes of the past. In November 1984 the *Galway Advertiser* presented special awards to commemorate the year and the two hurling recipients were Joe Salmon (left) and John Connolly (right), recognised as Galway's greatest hurling midfielders ever.

Parade Before National Hurling League Final of 1951 in New York's Polo Grounds
This is not the clearest photo but it represents the parade before the National Hurling
League final of 1951 in the Polo Grounds, New York when Galway defeated New York by
2-11 to 2-8. Leading the Galway team out is M.J. 'Inky' Flaherty (captain). Leading out
New York is the famous Terry Leahy (Kilkenny), who scored the winning point for
Kilkenny in the last minute of an epic All-Ireland Senior Hurling final against Cork in 1947.

First-ever Game Outside Connacht
The year was 1946 and the occasion the first-ever Hogan Cup semi-final in Fitzgerald
Stadium, Killarney when St Jarlath's College, Tuam defeated St Brendan's College,
Killarney by 2-14 to 2-4. FRONT FROM LEFT: Seán Keane, George Garvey, Dick Phillips,
Mick O'Malley, Tommy Lyons, Johnny Fitzpatrick, Seán Sheil, Jimmy Curran, Leo
Costelloe. BACK FROM LEFT: Christy Garvey, Ger McDonagh, Peter Solon, Tom Joyce,
Michael Greaney, Frank Mannion, Bartley Horan, Seán Purcell, Tommy Byrne, Joe
Keville, Geoffrey Prendergast.

Val Daly With Nestor Cup in 1986
The Connacht Senior Football Championship winners Cup
commemorates J.J. Nestor of Dunmore, who gave a lifetime
of service to the game of gaelic football in Galway as a player
and administrator. Here Val Daly (captain) raises the J.J.
Nestor Cup aloft in McHale Park, Castlebar after leading
Galway to success over Mayo by 0-8 to 0-7.

Joe Greaney v Éamonn Grimes 1979
This fine action shot shows Joe Greaney controlling the *sliotar* opposed by Éamonn Grimes of Limerick in a National Hurling League semi-final in Thurles in April 1979. Galway won that game by 1-15 to 4-5. Tipperary subsequently beat Galway in the National Hurling League final by 3-15 to 0-8.

Salthill Under-15 Óg Spórt 7-a-side Champions of Ireland 1979
FRONT FROM LEFT: Liam Wade, Paul Brennan, Niall O'Gorman, Ronan Mee, Jarlath O'Gara. BACK FROM LEFT: Jerome McDonagh, Rory Griffin, Liam Sammon (coach), John O'Grady, Ronan Fitzgerald, Pádhraic Timon. This victory among others set the scene for many further honours in the subsequent years.

Linking the All-Ireland Senior Hurling Wins of 1923, 1980 and 1987
This historic photograph taken in 1987 links three Galway All-Ireland Senior Hurling winning teams. FROM LEFT: Jim Power (member of 1923 team), Joe Cooney (1987) and Joe Connolly who captained the 1980 team — a total span of 64 years.

Dunmore MacHales — Galway Senior Football Champions of 1912
Our oldest photograph so far. FRONT FROM LEFT: Jimmy Mannion, Gerald Feeney (with ball), Pat Healy. CENTRE FROM LEFT: Martin Reddington, Tom Flaherty, Larry Rodgers, Larry Howley, unidentified, Ned Patton, Paddy Concannon. BACK FROM LEFT: Senator Frank Hugh O'Donnell (with bowtie), Paddy Mannion, Pat Togher (behind Mannion), Paddy Glennon, Ned Kilkenny, Tim Patton (behind Kilkenny), Martin Rodgers, Mick Halliday, Mick Farrell.

The Duggans of College Road
This photo of the three Duggan brothers Jimmy, Paddy and Seán, all of whom played Senior Hurling for Liam Mellowes, Galway and Connacht, was taken at the Liam Mellowes Hurling Club dinner in 1999. Paddy died later that year. This photo was the last one taken of all three maestros enjoying themselves on a social occasion.

UCG — Sigerson Cup Champions 1984
FRONT FROM LEFT: Harry Walsh, Pádhraic Duffy, Anthony Finnerty, Tomás Tierney (captain), Hughie Heskin, Tommy Carr, Michael Brennan. BACK FROM LEFT: Brian O'Donnell, Jim Egan, Peter Heffernan, James Reidy, Seán Twomey, John Maughan, Shay Fahy, Pádhraic 'Dandy' Kelly (RIP). The team coach was Tony Regan, former Roscommon and Combined Universities star.

Action from Connacht Senior Football Championship Final of 1984
This action picture from the Connacht Senior Football final of 1984 at Pearse Stadium, Salthill, shows Pat O'Neill of Tuam Stars clearing with his Mayo opponent Anthony Finnerty lying on the ground. Galway won that game by 2-13 to 2-9.

Galway's First and Only Senior All-Ireland Camogie Cup
Imelda Hobbins, the captain, holds the O'Duffy Cup (Senior Inter-county Camogie) in triumph after leading her team to All-Ireland victory in Croke Park in September 1996. Galway won the final against Cork by 4-8 to 1-15.

Mattie McDonagh — Most Be-medalled of all Galway stars

Mattie McDonagh has won four All-Ireland Senior Football Championship medals and ten Connacht Senior Football Championship medals, both records for a Connacht man. He also has the distinction of playing Minor football for Galway and in the same year of 1954 played Minor hurling for Roscommon (Ballygar played their hurling in County Roscommon then).

Galway's First-ever All-Ireland Under-21 Champions of 1972
FRONT FROM LEFT: Luke Glynn, Liam Shiel (RIP), Ned Campbell, Michael Coen, Iggy Clarke (captain), Tom Donoghoe, Tony Brehony and Marty Barrett. BACK FROM LEFT: Gerry Kelly, Gerry Glynn, Gerry Holland, Frank Donoghue, Andy Fenton, Michael Donoghue, Frank Burke. In the final played at Limerick's Gaelic Grounds Galway beat Dublin by 2-9 to 1-10.

Tomás Tierney Fields High in Connacht Final 1982
Tomás Tierney fields high for Galway in the 1982 Connacht Senior Football final against Mayo in Tuam, opposed by Tom Reilly (Mayo number 13) while Stephen Kinneavy (Galway number 3) and Jimmy Maughan (Mayo number 11) await the outcome. Galway ran away with that final on the score 3-17 to 0-10.

Celebration of 1956 All-Ireland in Grand Hotel Malahide
This photograph was taken at the banquet on 7 October 1956 to celebrate the All-Ireland football win earlier. FRONT FROM LEFT: Billy O'Neill, Toddy Ryan (masseur), Frank Stockwell, Jack Mahon, Jack Kissane, Seán Keeley (injured jaw). BACK FROM LEFT: Aidan Swords, Mattie McDonagh, Mick Greally, Jack Mangan (captain), Fr Paddy Mahon (chairman), Tom Dillon, Gerry Daly, Seán Purcell, Gerry Kirwan. Note all the Pioneer Pins.

The Joy and the Ecstasy!
Conor Hayes, the winning Galway captain (Senior Hurling), being mobbed by an army of joyous supporters as he leaves the old Hogan Stand after being presented with the Liam McCarthy Cup in 1987.

Presentation of All-Ireland Minor Football Medals in 1960
This photograph records the presentation of the All-Ireland Minor Football Championship medals in Ballygar in 1960. Here Fr Paddy Mahon (Chairman) presents Seán Cleary, the captain, with his medal. SEATED FROM LEFT ARE: Jack Whelan (Secretary County Board), Johnny Cotter (Vice Chairman Football Board), Brendan Nestor, John Dunne (Secretary) and Dr M.I. Mooney. Another of the winning minors, Noel Tierney, faces the camera.

Sarsfield (Bullaun-New Inn) All-Ireland S.H. Club Winners 1993
FRONT FROM LEFT: Donal Keane, Aidan Donohue, Pakie Cooney, Peter Kelly, Pádhraic Kelly, Michael McGrath, Willie Earls, Michael Kenny. BACK FROM LEFT: Michael Cooney, Joe McGrath, Peter Cooney, Tommy Kenny, Joe Cooney, Brendan Cooney, Noel Morrissey. The five Cooneys are all brothers.

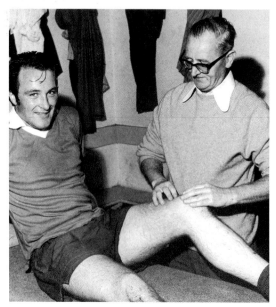

Freddie Smyth, the Masseur, Easing Weary Aches
Freddie Smyth of Gort was a very popular masseur with the Galway football teams of the 1970s. Here he eases the aches of staunch full-back Jack Cosgrave in the build-up to the All-Ireland final of 1974 against Dublin.

Cormac O'Donovan Chaired Off in 1992
Galway's All-Ireland Minor Hurling Championship captain Cormac O'Donovan being chaired off by delighted fans after being presented with the *Irish Press* Cup in Croke Park in September 1992. In the final Galway defeated Waterford by 1-13 to 2-4 to win their third ever All-Ireland Minor crown.

Geraghty Punches Clear

An action shot from a National Football League semi-final between Galway and Down in Croke Park in 1965 in which Johnny Geraghty punches clear, closely attended by Noel Tierney (number 3) and Enda Colleran (number 2) with Jackie Fitzsimons (Down) in close attendance. Galway went on to win the league that year.

Galway's All-Ireland Minor Champion Team of 1999

FRONT FROM LEFT: Kevin Brady, David Forde, Richard Murray, Ronan Reilly, John Culkin (captain), Johnny O'Loughlin, Cathal Coen. BACK FROM LEFT: Brian O'Mahony, Damian Hayes, Hugh Whoriskey, Fergal Moore, Conor Dervan, Michael John Quinn, Ger Farragher, Michael Coughlan. This was Galway's fourth Minor Hurling Championship success and they beat Tipperary in the final by 0-13 to 0-10.

Galway Connacht Final Winning Team of 1974
FRONT FROM LEFT: Johnny Hughes, Billy Joyce, Jarlath Burke (RIP), Gay Mitchell (captain), Coleen McDonagh, John Tobin. BACK FROM LEFT: Jack Cosgrave, T.J. Gilmore, Pat Sands, Liam O'Neill, Jimmy Duggan, Liam Sammon, Joe Waldron, Michael Geraghty, Tom Naughton. In that Connacht final at Pearse Stadium, Salthill, Galway defeated Roscommon by 2-14 to 0-8.

1976 Galway v Wexford Senior Hurling
Another action shot from the1976 drawn semi-final against Wexford in Páirc Uí Chaoimh, Cork. P.J. Qualter, the Galway full forward, is surrounded by Wexford's Willie Murphy and T. O'Connor before a capacity attendance on a gloriously sunny August day.

Action from 1978 Connacht Senior Football Championship Final in Pearse Stadium
A fine action shot of Roscommon's Michael Finneran rounding M.J. Judge (Galway) and Séamus McHugh in the 1978 Connacht final at Pearse Stadium, Salthill, when Roscommon defeated Galway by 2-7 to 0-9.

John Culkin Raises Irish Press Cup Aloft in 1999
John Culkin, the Galway All-Ireland winning Minor Hurling captain, raises the *Irish Press* Cup aloft after being presented with it by the GAA's patron, Dr Clifford, Archbishop of Cashel.

Joe Salmon — Was He Galway's Greatest Hurler?

Joe Salmon of Meelick–Eyrecourt was one of the most stylish hurlers ever to play for Galway. He was an outstanding midfielder in the 1940s and 1950s and in his latter days won fame as midfielder for the great Glen Rovers (Cork) club team.

Sr Loyola's Miraculous Medals

Sr Loyola (Presentation Sisters, Tuam) is the nun who supplied the miraculous medals to be sewn on the jerseys of the Galway footballers for the All-Ireland Senior football final of 1998 in which Galway beat Kildare. Here she is photographed with Nuala Kelly, holding the Sam Maguire Cup, on the occasion of the opening of the Seán Purcell and Frank Stockwell new roads in Tuam in 1999.

Iggy Clarke on Solo in 1978 Semi-final

The occasion was the All-Ireland semi-final (Senior Hurling) of 1978 in which Kilkenny beat Galway by 4-20 to 4-13. Here Iggy Clarke with ball on stick and an unusual number 5 on his back, races ahead of Kilkenny's Kevin Fennelly. Iggy usually played at number 7 — left half-back.

Galway — Connacht Senior Football Champions of 1966
FRONT FROM LEFT: Pat Donnellan, John Keenan, Cyril Dunne, Enda Colleran (captain), Jimmy Duggan, John Donnellan, Liam Sammon. BACK FROM LEFT: Séamus Leydon, Noel Tierney, Tom Brennan, Michael Moore, Mattie McDonagh, Mick Reynolds, Bosco McDermott, Tom Sands. In this epic game Galway beat Mayo in Castlebar by 0-12 to 1-8 and later went on to complete the three-in-a-row in All-Ireland finals.

The Johnny Flaherty Goal Which Beat Galway in 1981
How Offaly's Johnny Flaherty palmed the winning goal in the dying moments of the 1981 All-Ireland Senior Hurling final has always been a source of debate in Galway. Here is the drama unfolding as he palms the ball surrounded by Séamus Coen (left) and goalkeeper Michael Conneely (in white on right).

St Jarlath's First-ever Hogan Cup Champions of 1946–47
SEATED ON GROUND FROM LEFT: Mick Flanagan, Paddy Hoare, Seán Masterson.
KNEELING FROM LEFT: Seán Kavangh, Stephen Jordan, Anthony Morrison, Peter Solon,
Vincent McHale (captain), Seán Sheil, Billy Flynn, Mick Finnegan. BACK FROM LEFT:
Tommy Lyons, Colm Canavan, Mick O'Malley, Pat Flanagan, Tom Joyce, Tom Langan,
T.J. McHale, Christy McHale, Anthony O'Toole, John Joe Craughwell, Seán Masterson,
Seán Purcell. St Jarlath's beat St Patrick's, Armagh in the final at Croke Park by 4-10 to
3-8.

'The Master' in Action
This fine action shot of Seán
Purcell ('The Master') in full
flight captures the style and
skill of a man recognised as
Ireland's greatest ever Gaelic
footballer. The year was 1956
(March)   in   the   annual
Combined Universities (white
jersey) versus Ireland game in
Croke Park. FROM LEFT: Gerry
O'Malley (CU), Paddy Casey
(Ireland), Seán Purcell (CU).

Castlegar County Senior Champions 1936–1940
FRONT FROM LEFT: Staff McDermott, John Corcoran, Stephen Corcoran. Mascot: J. Corcoran. CENTRE FROM LEFT: Paddy McDermott, Paddy Melvin, John Corcoran, Michael O'Brien, Willie Cullinan, John McGrath. BACK FROM LEFT: Jim Donoghue, Tom Molloy, Stephen Hosty, Tom Casserly, Mick Gilmore, Stephen Fahy, John King, Matt Hackett (only togged-out players identified).

Joe Corcoran Chaired Off — Croke Park in 1970
Joe Corcoran (Galway All-Ireland Minor) captain of 1970 being chaired from Croke Park after defeating Kerry in a final replay at Croke Park by 1-11 to 1-10. On the left with his right hand stretched high is his old friend, the late Seán Callaghan, while helping to carry him off in triumph is one of his minor colleagues, Tom Naughton.

Noel Lane Chaired Off in Triumph in 1985

The occasion was a very wet day in Croke Park in 1985 when Galway defeated Cork in the All-Ireland Senior Hurling semi-final by 4-12 to 5-5. Here Noel Lane, one of Galway's stars, is carried in triumph after the game by ecstatic Galway supporters including Miko Donoghoe (on right), former hurling board official.

The late Pádhraic 'Dandy' Kelly in Action in 1983

This is a fine action shot of Pádhraic 'Dandy' Kelly of Galway racing past Donegal's Michael Carr in the 1983 All-Ireland semi-final, won by Galway by 1-12 to 1-11. There was genuine grief in Galway in November 2001 when 'Dandy' died suddenly leaving a young wife, Jamie, and four young children.

Castlegar — County Minor Champions 1949
FRONT FROM LEFT: Christy Broderick, John J. Wall, Paddy Coyne, Pádraic Nolan, Michael Connell, Billy Talbot, Willie Fahy, Tommy J. Broderick. BACK FROM LEFT: James King, Tommy Fahy, Pat Shaughnessy, Tim Lally, Séamus Cullinane, Paddy Giles, Stephen Healy, Timmy Kelly.

Dining on SS Ryndam From New York to Cóbh in 1957
We had the best of food on board the SS Ryndam en route from New York to Cóbh in November 1957. The Galway players photographed are Séamus Colleran, Mick Greally, Jack Mahon and Jackie Coyle (RIP), with two Dutch waiters at the ready.

Gaelic Park New York 1957
The Galway Team which beat New York in a challenge game on Sunday 27 October 1957.
FRONT FROM LEFT: Jack Mahon, Liam Mannion, Seán Keeley, Mattie Mannion, Gerry
Daly, Jack Mangan (captain), Jackie Coyle (RIP), Aidan Swords (RIP). BACK FROM
LEFT: Rev Mattie Walsh (Chairman County Board), Jimmy Staunton (Hartford), Seán
Purcell, Séamus Colleran, Joe Young, Mick Greally, Jack Kissane, Gerry Kirwan, Tom
McHugh, Johnny Cotter (Vice-Chairman Galway Football Board).

Old Soldiers Never Die — They Simply Fade Away
At half time in the 1988 Galway County Senior Football Championship final, the living members of the 1938 All-Ireland Senior Football Championship winning team were introduced and received an ovation in Tuam Stadium. FROM LEFT: 'Small' Pat McDonagh, Master Raftery representing his grand-dad Mick, Dinny O'Sullivan, Jimmy McGauran, Bobby Beggs, Paddy Mitchell, Jimmy Greaney, Dermot Mitchell, Mick Ryder, John 'Tull' Dunne.

Pre All-Ireland Snapshot From 1956
In those days, almost 50 years ago, we depended mostly on the print media for publicity prior to an All-Ireland final. This is a lovely shot of three of Galway's 1956 team — all officers in the Irish Army in An Chéad Chath Renmore. FROM LEFT: Joe Young, Billy O'Neill and Jack Kissane (seated).

Galway County GAA Board Personel 1979
FRONT FROM LEFT: Mark Heneghan, Mick Sylver, Norman Farragher (Chairman), John Dunne, David McGann (Secretary), M.J. 'Inky' Flaherty. BACK FROM LEFT: Pa Burke, Tom Cunningham, Joe McDonagh, Noel Treacy, Maitias Mac Donnchadha, Brendan Murphy, Frank Corcoran, John Molloy (PRO).

Action From 1983 All-Ireland Senior Hurling Championship Semi-final Galway v Cork
Dermot McCurtain (Cork) gets possession ahead of Galway's Joe Connolly in this fine action shot from a game in which Cork defeated Galway by 5-14 to 1-16 on Sunday 7 August 1983.

Enjoying His Solo Against Toomevara in 1994

This is Michael 'Bottler' Kenny soloing through the Toomevara defence in the 1994 All-Ireland Senior Hurling club final won by his club, Sarsfields, on the score 1-14 to 3-6. How did he get the name 'Bottler'? It seems as a youngster he used to help stack bottles in Wards of Ballyfa.

Annaghdown, Galway Senior Football Champions of 1987 (Club Centenary Year)
FRONT FROM LEFT: Gerry Lardner, Paddy J. Burke, Michael Greaney, Gerry Forde, Willie Hughes (captain), Michael Burke, Brendan Melia. BACK FROM LEFT: Gerry Scully, Brendan Corbett, P.J. Fallon, Michael Cahill, Gerry Keane, Frank Broderick, Myles Meehan, Michael Melia, Tom Naughton. In the final they defeated Milltown by 1-7 to 0-7.

Galway v Dublin in Croke Park National Football League 1959 (1 March)
It was a sunny frosty March day and over 39,000 attended a classic game won by Dublin 3-10 to 3-6. FRONT FROM LEFT: Liam Mannion, Jack Mahon, Seán Purcell, 'Hauleen' McDonagh, Eddie Sharkey, Jackie Coyle, John Donnellan. BACK FROM LEFT: Mick Greally, Brendan Glynn, Seán Meade, Patsy Coyle, Paddy Dunne, Joe Young, Jack Kissane, Séamus Colleran.

Action From Galway Senior Hurling Championship game 1979 — Gort v Kinvara
This action shot from 1979 sees Gerry Fahy of Gort (left) in action against Mick Curtin of Kinvara. Galway Senior Hurling Championship games attracted huge crowds over the years.

Action From Galway v Down (Senior Football) All-Ireland Semi-final 1959

It was Down's first All-Ireland Senior Football semi-final in Croke Park. Here Pat Rice clears the ball watched by Joe Young (Galway), James McCartan (Down, with cap), George Lavery (Down), referee Tadhg Crowley (Cork, in background), 'Hauleen' McDonagh (Galway), Jackie Coyle (Galway) and Kevin Mussen (Down). Galway won the game 1-11 to 1-4, but it was no walkover.

Cardinal Spelman (New York) throws in the *sliotar* to start the National Hurling League final Galway v New York Polo Grounds 1951. This was the old style throw-in to start a game, eight facing eight. The two captains are at the head of their lines, Terry Leahy (New York in white) and M.J. 'Inky' Flaherty (Galway number 14). Galway won this game 2-11 to 2-8.

Irish Nationwide Honours Three-in-a-row Stars in Croke Park 1989

For the past few decades Irish Nationwide Building Society honours a team from the past on All-Ireland days. In 1989 (25 years on from 1964) they honoured Galway's three-in-a-row (1964–66) men. Here the former players are in jovial mood: from left Tom Sands, Kieran O'Connor, Michael Moore, Liam Sammon, John Keenan, Seán Cleary, Christy Tyrrell and Séamus Leydon.

Galway Connacht Final Winning Team of 1973

This the Galway Senior Football team which beat Mayo in the Connacht final at Castlebar by 1-17 to 2-12. FRONT FROM LEFT: Brendan Colleran, Johnny Hughes, Billy Joyce, Liam Sammon, Johnny Coughlan, Maurice Burke, Michael Rooney. BACK FROM LEFT: Liam O'Neill, Jack Cosgrave, T.J. Gilmore, Jimmy Duggan, Gay Mitchell, Joe Waldron, John Tobin, Tom Naughton.

Macnas Honours Three-in-a-row in 1987 Connacht Final

Twenty-one years after winning the three-in-a-row in 1966, Macnas, under Ollie Jennings, honoured the achievement with their own depiction of the team in a Parade on Connacht final day 1987 in Castlebar. Here they are with Johnny Geraghty leading Enda Colleran (hidden), Noel Tierney, Bosco McDermott, John Donnellan, Seán Meade, Martin Newell, Pat Donnellan, Mick Garrett, Cyril Dunne, Mattie McDonagh, Séamus Leydon, Christie Tyrrell, Sean Cleary and John Keenan.

Galway's First and Only All-Ireland Senior Camogie Champions 1996

FRONT FROM LEFT: Carmel Hannon, Veronica Curtin, Imelda Hobbins, (captain), Martina Harkin, Dympna Maher, Denise Gilligan. BACK FROM LEFT: Ann Broderick, Pamela Nevin, Louise Curry, Olive Costello, Sharon Glynn, Olivia Broderick. The two mascots in front are Karen Kennedy and Ciara Ward.

Galway's Four National Football League Captains Together in 1981
This photograph hangs in the Sacre Coeur Hotel, Salthill where it was taken in 1981. Galway have won four National Football League titles. The four captains are, from left: Barry Brennan (1980–1981), John 'Tull' Dunne (1939–1940), Jack Mahon (1956–1957) and John Donnellan (1964–1965). A historic photo.

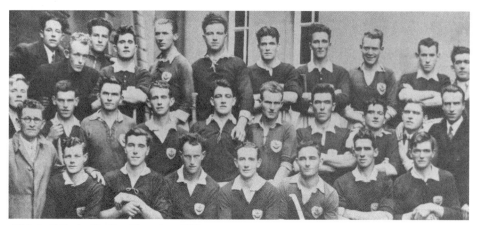

All-Ireland Junior Hurling Champions 1959
SEATED FROM LEFT: Tommie Cunningham, Ardrahan; Walter Connolly, Gort; Tom Lambert, Kilbeacanty; Joe Costello (First Army Battalion) captain; Paddy Forde, Ballinasloe; James Curley, Clontuskert; Michael Mulryan, Castlegar. STANDING FROM LEFT: J. Faherty, J. Whelan, secretary of the Galway County Board GAA; Joe Hanney, Killimor; Mattie Leary, Ardrahan; Joe Hanniffy, Maree; Bob Forde, Kinvara, Patrick Fahy, sub-goalie, Kilbeacanty; Joe Muldoon, Kinvara. BACK FROM LEFT: first man not identified, Joe Darcy, Ballinakill; Malachy Donnellan, Maree; Willie Donnellan, Maree; Jack Beehan, Cappataggle; Jack Fahy, Kilbeacanty; Eamon Hogan, Woodford; Willie Niland, Clarenbridge; Joe Cooney, Paterswell; Martin Lowry, Mullagh; last man not identified. Galway beat London in the final 2-6 to 2-2.

Galway National Hurling League Champions 1951
This photograph was taken in Croke Park at the 1951 All-Ireland Senior Hurling semi-final in which Galway were defeated by Wexford 3-11 to 2-9. FRONT FROM LEFT: Jack Whelan (secretary County Board), Kieran McNamee, Mickey Glynn, Josie Gallagher, Joe Salmon, Tadhg Kelly, Mickey Burke, Hugh Gordon, Miko McInerney. BACK FROM LEFT: Paddy Ruane (official), Seán Duggan, M.J. Flaherty, Colm Corless, Jimmy Brophy, Johnny Molloy, Frank Flynn, Tommy Moroney, Mick Sylver (official)

Galway's Only Goal Against Kerry in 1959 Final
Over 84,000 people thronged Croke Park for this final. Though scores were level 0-7 to 1-4 entering the last quarter, Kerry won well in the end, 3-7 to 1-4. Here Frank Evers (number 8) scores Galway's only goal beating Kerry goalkeeper Johnny Cullotty, with from left: Frank Stockwell (Galway), Tim 'Tiger' Lyons (Kerry), Mick Laide (Galway) as Niall Sheehy and Jerome O'Shea (both Kerry) collide trying to stop Frank's shot.

The Burial of Brendan Nestor 1981

Brendan Nestor was one of Galway's greatest ever corner forwards and later an outstanding official. He played club football with Erin's Hopes and Geraldines in Dublin and later with his native Dunmore McHales. They came from near and far to his funeral. The guard of honour on the left is led by well-known Cork official Denis Conroy. Following the hearse are his sons Tom and Jim and to their left are Murt Kelly and Joe Keohane of Kerry.

Action from 2001 All-Ireland Senior Hurling Final Galway v Tipperary

This fine action shot shows Joe Rabbitte with the *sliotar* in his left hand bursting through the Tipperary defence with team-mate Mark Kerins backing him up. Tipperary won the final 2-18 to 2-15.

Champions of Connacht 1938

The Galway 1938 Senior Football team which won the All-Ireland. The photograph was taken on the occasion of the Connacht final against Mayo at St Coman's Park, Roscommon, which Galway won by 0-8 to 0-5. FRONT FROM LEFT: Mickey Mannion, Mick Rafftery, Bobby Beggs, Frank Cunniffe, Jackie Flavin, John Dunne, Eugene O'Sullivan, Dinny Sullivan. BACK FROM LEFT: Dr M.B. Farrell, Jimmy McGauran, Mick Connaire, Ned Mulholland, Charlie Connolly, John Burke, Martin Kelly, Brendan Nestor, Jack Whelan (secretary Galway County Board) and J.J. Nestor (Chairman Galway Football Board).

Action From Galway v Mayo Senior Football Championship Game Tuam 1954

Galway caused a major upset in this game, beating Mayo, the 1954 National Football League champions. Here Iggy Hanniffy (Galway number 2) rises for the ball with, from left, Mick Flanagan (Mayo), Tom Langan (Mayo), Tom Dillon (Galway), Dan O'Neill (Mayo); Jack Mahon (Galway) and Frank Leonard (Mayo) looking on.

Action From 1987 Senior Hurling Final

Brilliant action shot of Liam Fennelly (Kilkenny) with *sliotar* glued to stick running past opponent Conor Hayes in the All-Ireland Senior Hurling final of 1987, won by Galway on the score 1-12 to 0-9.

Galway March Out Against Kerry in 1984 Semi-final

The march round after the Artane Boys' Band is a Croke Park ritual. Séamus McHugh (captain) leads Galway out against Kerry in the1984 All-Ireland Senior Football semi-final followed by Pat Comer, Joe Kelly, Pádhraic Moran, Pat O'Neill, Tomás Tierney. Paudie O'Shea leads the Kerry men in the picture. Kerry won by 2-17 to 0-11.

Tony Doran v Joe McDonagh

Two famous names in the GAA battle it out in an epic 1976 Senior Hurling semi-final game, Galway v Wexford, in sun-drenched Páirc Uí Chaomh. Pádhraic Puirséal (*Irish Press*) called Doran 'the man from Boolavogue'. McDonagh was later one of the GAA's most popular Presidents.

Galway's 1948 Galway Senior Football Team Against Roscommon

This photograph (the property of Seán Purcell) is one of the few which includes the great duo Ned Keogh and Tom Sullivan together. FRONT FROM LEFT: Pat McManus, John Glynn, Frank Stockwell, Jarlath Canavan, Seán Purcell, Seán Thornton, Pat Ryan. BACK FROM LEFT: Brendan Hanniffy, Frank Quinn, Jack Mangan, Tom Connern, Joe Duggan, Eddie Condon, Ned Keogh, Tom Sullivan.

Another Fine Hurling Shot of the Ball on Stick Solo from 1981 All-Ireland Final

Two great artists battle it out in the 1981 Senior Hurling final. Finbarr Gantly, with ball on stick, is followed by Offaly's great defender Ger Coughlan. Offaly won their first Senior Hurling Championship that day by 2-12 to 0-15.

Mattie McDonagh Admires Sam at Player Wills Reception 1965

In the 1960s Player Wills used to host a reception at their HQ on the South Circular Road on the Monday after the All-Ireland final. Here Mattie McDonagh holds Sam with, from left: Patsy Geraghty (Galway official), Rev. P. Mahon (Chairman Galway Football Board) and Mr Boland of Player Wills.

The Night of the Long Wait

It took ages to get to Galway with the Liam McCarthy Cup in 1980 after a wait of fifty-seven long years. The team got seated in the Sacre Coeur Hotel, Salthill at 3.00am on the Tuesday morning after the game. Seated before the meal began are, FROM LEFT: Cathy Griffin, now Joe Connolly's wife, Joe the captain, Mr O'Flaherty and his wife Bridie, then Mayor of Galway. STANDING FROM LEFT: David McGann (Chairman Galway County Board), Seán Dunleavy (Sacre Coeur) and Dr Éamonn Casey, Bishop of Galway.

Launching of Galway's First-ever GAA Yearbook in 1965
FRONT FROM LEFT: Rev. P. Mahon, Pat Donnellan, Jack Mahon, (co-ordinating editor), Rev. Brendan Kavanagh, An t-Athair Leon Ó Morcháin. BACK FROM LEFT: Eddie Gibson, Jimmy Duggan, Rev T. Tarpey and Joe Burke. The Yearbook was launched in the Salthill Hotel.

Old Soldiers — Great Friends
You need to look at the top photograph on page 2 to appreciate this one. The first photograph showed these great opponents in aerial duel in 1972. Now nine years later, after Galway defeated Roscommon in the National Football League final in Croke Park by 1-11 to 1-3, Dermot Earley (number 12) shakes the hand of opponent Billy Joyce. Old foes but old friends too.

John Connolly v Eugene Coughlan in 1981 final

Yet another fine action shot from the 1981 final won by Offaly for their first national crown in Senior Hurling. Here Eugene Coughlan, a fine full-back, sticks to John Connolly and the *sliotar* closely.

St Jarlath's College, Tuam, Hogan Cup Champions 1960

FRONT FROM LEFT: Johnny Geraghty, Peter Crisham, Gerry Prendergast, Pat Sheridan (captain), Séamus Kilraine, Séamus Sanderson, Larry O'Brien. CENTRE FROM LEFT: Seán Brennan, Anthony Jordan, Joe Jennings, Séamus Leydon, Gay Nicholson, Liam Campbell, Peadar McGee, Jimmy Walsh, Pat Donnellan. BACK FROM LEFT: Enda Colleran, Padhraic Forde, John Morley, Vincent Greaney, Vincent McGagh, Eddie Geraghty, Tony Ryan, Michael Staunton.

Action from 1971 Senior Hurling Semi-final Galway v Tipperary
The venue was Birr. Tipperary won a high scoring game by 3-26 to 6-8. Here Pádhraic Fahy (Galway) with *sliotar* in left hand tries to outwit Mick Roche (Tipperary) on left with Tadhg O'Connor (Tipperary's captain) racing in to help.

Galway's All-Ireland Champions (Senior Football) of 1966
FRONT FROM LEFT: Seán Cleary, Coleen McDonagh, Cyril Dunne, Martin Newell, Enda Colleran (captain), Johnny Geraghty, Jimmy Duggan, Pat Donnellan. BACK FROM LEFT: Séamus Leydon, Noel Tierney, Seán Meade, Mattie McDonagh, Liam Sammon, John Keenan, Bosco McDermott. Galway beat Meath in the 1966 final by 1-10 to 0-7.

Were You There in 1971?
At the drawn Connacht Senior Football Championship final between Sligo and Galway in 1971 a section of the crowd, mostly youngsters, encroached onto the field of play in Castlebar and the game finished out in a welter of excitement. Were you part of the crowd on that occasion? The final score was 2-15 apiece.

Galway All-Ireland Minors in Independent House (1952)

There wasn't much made of Minors who won All-Irelands 50 years ago. No team photo or presentation of a cup then. On the day after Galway beat Cavan by 2-9 to 1-6 to win the Tom Markham Cup for the first time, they visited Independent House. Front shows Rev P. Mahon, Michael Ryan the goalie (with flag), Brian Mahon (captain), Liam Manning, Patsy Geraghty, John Dunne (hat) and the team party.

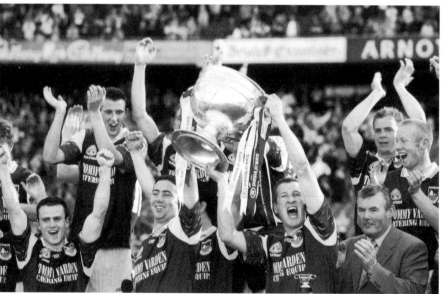

Winning Sam in 2001

We must keep up with the times. Gary Fahey (captain) and Kieran Comer (previous captain) hold Sam aloft in Croke Park on All-Ireland day 2001 after defeating Meath by 0-17 to 0-8. Others in front are Derek Savage and Seán McCague (President CLG). At back Tomás Mannion, Joe Bergin, Michael Donnellan and Michael Comer.

Where Are They Now?
Labane National School County School's Camogie Champions of 1991. FRONT FROM LEFT: Crona Winston, Andreena Fahy, Caitriona Fahy, Mairéad Mahony. BACK FROM LEFT: Jean Tannian, Caoimhe Burke, Aoife Winston (captain), Fidelma Coyne (B.Ed coach), Valerie Tannian, Elaine Cannon, Jacinta Fahy.

Rooney Goals v Mayo in Castlebar (Connacht Senior Football final 1973)
Michael Rooney (Cortoon Shamrocks) shoots past J.J. Costelloe (Mayo) in the Connacht Senior Football final of 1973. He is pursued by Johnny Carey, with Ray Niland (17) looking on. Galway defeated Mayo that day by 1-17 to 2-12.

St Raphael's College Loughrea — First-ever Three-in-a-row of Senior (A) Colleges Camogie Titles
FRONT FROM LEFT: Clare Robinson, Mary Dolphin, Deirdre Costello, Breege Stratford (captain), Imelda Hobbins, Anne Bugler, Aideen Murphy, Cora Curley. CENTRE FROM LEFT: Angela Cooney, Anne Fahy, Eilís Kilkenny, Ger Fahy, Fionnuala Keane, Olive Costello, Brigid Fahy. BACK FROM LEFT: Annette Regan, Tríona Dolphin, Carmel Ryan, Caroline Loughnane, Rita Dolan, Marlene Linnane, Sharon Maher. The College went on to win a record seven-in-a-row of Camogie Senior titles.

Galway Minor All-Ireland Final Champions 1960.
FRONT FROM LEFT: Johnny Gavin, Enda Colleran, Gabriel Lohan, Christy Tyrrell, Seán Cleary (captain) Gerry Prendergast, Éamonn Slattery, Andy Donnelly. BACK FROM LEFT: Michael King, Larry O'Brien, Johnny Smith, Séamus Leydon, Harry Anderson, Noel Tierney, Tony Ryan. This team had big wins over all comers en route to the final in which they beat Cork easily by 4-9 to 1-5.

Moll an Óige agus Tiocfaidh Sí

Mullagh Under-10 Camogie Champions for two-in-a-row in 1987. FRONT FROM LEFT: Linda Connaughton, Aileen Hardiman, Laura Fallon, Georgina Reilly. CENTRE FROM LEFT: Teresa Garvey, Rosa Clarke, Claire Fahy, Ruth Cahalan (captain), Mary Mitchell, Olivia Coen, Sarah Kelly. BACK FROM LEFT: Emer Connolly, Elma Rafferty, Ann Garvey, Ann Hardiman, Sarah Donohoe, Geraldine Donohoe, Nicola Reilly, Michelle Walsh, Mairéad Mitchell.

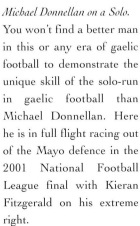

Michael Donnellan on a Solo.
You won't find a better man in this or any era of gaelic football to demonstrate the unique skill of the solo-run in gaelic football than Michael Donnellan. Here he is in full flight racing out of the Mayo defence in the 2001 National Football League final with Kieran Fitzgerald on his extreme right.

Connacht Colleges Senior (A) Hurling Champions 1991 St Raphael's Loughrea.
FRONT FROM LEFT: Maurice Murray, John Flanagan, Alan Curley, Keith Finnerty (captain), Francis Keane, Paul O'Loughlin, John Murray. CENTRE FROM LEFT: James Spellman, Martin Dolan, John Magee, Pat Dillon, Kevin Boyle, Pat O'Connor, Seán Forde, David Keane. BACK FROM LEFT: Des Keary, Thomas Kavanagh, Austin Mahony, Conor Reynolds, Paul Cleary, Oliver Briscoe, Eddie Corban.

Jimmy Duggan Injured in Exchanges Against Offaly in the All-Ireland Senior Football Final 1971.

Exchanges were rugged betimes in the 1971 All-Ireland Senior Football final, Galway v Offaly, won by Offaly (their first-ever title) 1-14 to 2-8. Here Jimmy Duggan (Galway) is prostrate after a clash. Photograph also includes from left, Michael Rooney (Galway), Emmet Farrell (Galway number 13), Offaly goalkeeper Martin Furlong, Paddy McCormack (Offaly number 3), and Michael Ryan (Offaly) seated on ground with ball.

Galway v Dublin National Hurling League 1963 in Croke Park
FRONT FROM LEFT: Jimmy Conroy, Ned Dervan, Joe Salmon, Mickey Cullinane, Jimmy Duggan, Joe Lyons, Mick Curtin. BACK FROM LEFT: Jackie Gill, Michael Cullinane, Packie Burke, Michael Regan, Séamus Gohery, Jimmy Hegarty, Tim Sweeney, Tom Conway. This was before the goalkeeper was required to wear a distinctive jersey.

They Could March in 1956. Galway v Cork All-Ireland Senior Football Final
Leading Galway is captain Jack Mangan followed by Seán Keeley, Gerry Daly, Tom Dillon, Jack Kissane, Jack Mahon, Mick Greally, Frank Evers, Mattie McDonagh, Jackie Coyle, Billy O'Neill, Joe Young, Gerry Kirwan and Frank Stockwell. Seán Purcell is hidden behind Stockwell. The Corkman on the left is Paddy Harrington, father of renowned golfer Pádhraic Harrington.

The UCG Team Which Won the Fitzgibbon Cup in 1954
UCG defeated UCD in the final by 5-3 to 0-3 in Fahy's Field Galway. FRONT FROM LEFT:
Tommy O'Toole, Eddie Abberton, Albert Haverty, Séamus Trayers, Paddy O'Donoghue,
Noel McMahon, Sonny Fallon, Paddy Mannion, Maurice White. BACK FROM LEFT:
Stephen Carty (light overcoat), Gerry Meehan, Pat Shaughnessy, Philip Waldron, Eoin
Kelly, John Naughton, Eddie Fallon, Miko McInerney (head sideways), Tony O'Gorman,
H. O'Donnell, Frank Daly, Séamus Cullinane.

*Tom Sands Carried Off in Triumph
in 1972*
Fr Griffins had just won the
Galway   Senior   Football
Championship final in 1972,
defeating Tuam Stars by 4-10 to
2-7. Tom Sands holds the Frank
Fox Cup in his left hand to the
delight of supporters. The boy
on the right, John Hanniffy,
later played Minor Football for
Galway in the 1980s.

Joe Duffy in Action in Connacht Minor Football Final 1972

This action shot from the 1972 Connacht Minor Football final sees Joe Duffy in ballet fashion skipping over Roscommon's P. Kelly as M. Conroy (Galway) comes to aid Duffy. Galway won that final by 4-11 to 1-11 but later fell to Cork in the semi-final. Duffy now owns a thriving bar/restaurant in Chicago.

Action From 1975 All-Ireland Senior Hurling Final

This photograph captures the intensity of the midfield exchanges in a Senior Hurling final. The year was 1975. Galway were on the way up. Michael Connolly hits the *sliotar* as Kilkenny's Frank Cummins attempts to block. Kilkenny won that final by 2-22 to 2-10.

Galway's All-Ireland Winning Senior Football Team of 1934
FRONT FROM LEFT: 'Cussaun' Brennan, Dinny O'Sullivan, Mick Ferriter, Mick Higgins (captain, with mascot), Tadhg McCarthy, Dermot Mitchell, Brendan Nestor, Dick Kenny (team manager). BACK FROM LEFT: M. O'Regan (Secretary, with glasses), Frank Fox, Ralph Griffin, Martin Kelly, Hugo Carey, Mick Connaire, John 'Tull' Dunne, P.J. McDonnell, Tommy Hughes and Stephen Jordan TD, a well-known referee from Athenry who officiated in Croke Park earlier that day.

John Connolly Signing Autographs in 1980
Youngsters cram around John Connolly looking for an autograph after Galway won the All-Ireland Senior Hurling title in 1980. John is still associated with Galway hurling at club and county level.

Galway March Out in 1954 Senior Football Final
Croke Park was so different but crowded then as now. Mick Higgins leads his team out against Dublin followed by Mick Connaire, Hugo Carey, Brendan Nestor, Frank Fox, Dermot Mitchell, Tommy Hughes, Dinny O'Sullivan, 'Cussaun' Brennan, Martin Kelly, P.J. McDonnell, Tadhg McCarthy, Mick Ferriter and John Dunne. Ralph Griffin is hidden between Kelly and McDonnell.

Galway Minor Hurlers of 1973
FRONT FROM LEFT: Fred Power, Tom Murphy, Sylvie Linnane, Jackie Dervan, Brian Kelly, Eamonn Dooley, Michael Hanniffy. BACK FROM LEFT: Gerry Burke, Gerry Holian, John Donoghue, Gerry Maher, Frank Larkin, Hugh Silke, Gerry Cohan, Gerry Murphy. Kilkenny won that final by 4-5 to 3-7. Galway had still to win a minor title. This one was close.

Action from 1973 All-Ireland Senior Football Final
Brendan Colleran blocks off Jimmy Barry Murphy as Tommy Joe Gilmore and Declan
Barron (Cork) race ahead. Cork won the final by 3-17 to 2-13.

All-Stars All
At a celebration in Galway in 1985 to honour Galway's All-Star hurlers of that year. FRONT
FROM LEFT: Cyril Farrell (Galway's very successful team manager), Dr Mick Loftus
(Uachtarán CLG), John McNamara (Bank of Ireland). BACK FROM LEFT: Sylvie Linnane,
Joe Cooney, Conor Hayes, Brendan Lynskey, Séamus Coen.

Fielding High in Tuam, Galway v Mayo Connacht Senior Football Championship 1960
A Connacht Senior Football Championship first round game in Tuam, Galway v Mayo, always attracted a full house. Here Jack Mahon (4) is pictured fielding high as Tommie Treacy (Mayo number 13), Jimmy Farrell (goalkeeper, hands poised) and Seán Keeley look on.

Aerial Combat From 1980 Hurling Final Against Limerick
Where is the *sliotar* in this aerial clash of the ash? Noel Lane (15), Leonard Enright (Limerick number 3), John Connolly (14) and P.J. Molloy (12), with Frank Burke (extreme right) running in to help out.

Galway Senior Football Team Which Beat Cork (National Football League champions) in Clonakilty in 1952

FRONT FROM LEFT: Jack Mangan, Jimmy Ward, Iggy Hanniffy, Brian Mahon, Seán Purcell, Frank Stockwell, Tommy Brosnan, Gerry Kirwan. BACK FROM LEFT: Niall Sheridan, Peter O'Shea, Christy Dillon, Michael Ryan, Tom Dillon, Andy Joyce, Ger Colleran, Billy O'Neill, Vincent Lynch, Tom McHugh. Ryan, Mahon, Brosnan and Kirwan had won All-Ireland Minor medals a month previously.

Galway's All-Ireland Winning Junior Team of 1958

FRONT FROM LEFT: Tommy Fay, John Donnellan, Kevin Cummins, Michael Walsh, Liam Mannion (captain), John Glavey, Paddy Davin, Michael Costelloe. BACK FROM LEFT: Brian Geraghty, Eddie Sharkey, Jimmy Farrell, M. 'Hauleen' McDonagh, Andy O'Connor, Brian Naughton, Patsy Coyle, Seán Mannion, Frank Cloonan, Seán Meade, Paddy Dunne. Galway beat Meath in the home final and Lancashire in the final proper.

St Colman's Vocational School, Gort, Complete Vocational Schools' Collection
St Colman's, Gort, winners of the AIB Vocational Schools' Under-15 All-Ireland Hurling Championship in 1991. Since then all three second-level schools in Gort amalgamated to become Gort Community School. FRONT FROM LEFT: Declan Grimes, Patrick Carr, Colm Corless, Brian Murphy, Peter Cummins, Liam Corcoran, Michael McInerney, Brian Hession. CENTRE FROM LEFT: Finbar Gantly, Brendan Nestor, Niall Hynes, Liam Madden, Thomas Hall, Gerard Niland, Joseph Connolly, Declan Spain, Cyril Hession. BACK FROM LEFT: Gerard Moroney, Ronan O'Dea, Eoin O'Loughlin, Francis Comyn, Aidan Mullens (captain), Niall Linnane, Gerard Giblin, Brian Naughton, Tony Loughrey, Oliver Lyons, Thomas Fahy, Peter Linnane, Kevin Killoran, Shane Keane.

Action From 1987 Final. Sylvie Linnane v Harry Ryan of Kilkenny

Sylvie Linnane was an outstanding hurler with Gort and Galway. A great sticksman at cornerback, he took no prisoners. Here he clashes with immediate opponent Harry Ryan of Kilkenny in the 1987 All-Ireland Senior Hurling final. Ryan has the ball, whatever about the hurley.

The Captain's Handshake Before All-Ireland Senior Football Final 1971

Liam Sammon (Galway captain) shakes the hand of Willie Bryan (Offaly captain) before the 1971 final in Croke Park. It was won by Offaly, their first-ever Senior Football title, by 1-14 to 2-8. Paul Kelly (Dublin) the referee looks on.

Galway Minor Hurlers of 1987 Defeated by Tipperary in the All-Ireland Semi-final
FRONT FROM LEFT: Kenneth Kennedy, Brendan Uniacke, Pat Forde, Conor Molloy, Shane Kelly, Damien Curley, Murt Killilea. BACK FROM LEFT: Pádraig Kelly, Paul Hardiman, Richard Burke, Brian O'Donovan, Ger Keane, Justin Campbell, Michael 'Bomber' Killilee, Eamonn Dervan.

Presentation of Connacht Minor Championship Cup 1987
Dr Donal Keenan (Roscommon), former star Roscommon footballer and former Uachtarán CLG, presenting the Tom Kilcoyne Cup (Connacht Minor Football Championship) to Seán Óg Dunleavy (Galway captain) after Galway defeated Mayo by 2-8 to 2-4 in the Connacht Minor final.

Galway and Connacht Senior Hurling Club Champions 1972 — Castlegar

FRONT FROM LEFT: Br Noel Commins, Paddy Egan, Paddy Glynn, John Connolly, Mickey Connor, Tony Gavin, Pakie Connor. BACK FROM LEFT: Gerry Glynn, John Corcoran, Stephen Francis, Declan Furey, Tommy V. Broderick, Alfie Cooney, Ted Murphy, Tommy Glynn.

Action From 1973 Football Final Galway v Cork

Maurice Burke (Galway) on ball shadowed by dual Cork star Brian Murphy with Tom Naughton (Galway) and Humphrey Kelliher (Cork) running by.

Galway's Senior Hurling Team Defeated by Kilkenny in 1975 Senior Hurling Final
FRONT FROM LEFT: Pádhraic Lally, P.J. Molloy, Pádhraic Fahy, John Connolly, Gerry Coone, Marty Barrett, Niall McInerney. BACK FROM LEFT: Iggy Clarke, Seán Murphy, Seán Silke, P.J. Qualter, Mike Conneely, Frank Burke, Joe Clarke, Joe McDonagh.

John Purcell Holds Frank Fox Cup Aloft in 1989
John Purcell, son of Seán 'The Master', captained the Tuam Stars to Galway Senior Football Championship success in 1989 just as his father did before him in the 1950s. Briseann an dúchas tré shúilibh an chait.

Joe McDonagh Leads Galway Out in 1979 Senior Hurling Final Against Kilkenny
Joe McDonagh, later to become one of the GAA's outstanding Presidents, leads Galway out against Kilkenny in 1979 All-Ireland final, won by Kilkenny. He is followed by Séamus Shinnors, Niall McInerney, Steve Mahon, Andy Fenton, Finbar Gantly and Iggy Clarke.

Galway Football Team 1925 — All-Ireland Champions for the First Time
FRONT FROM LEFT: Harry Burke, Mick Walsh, Paddy Roche. CENTRE FROM LEFT: Mick Bannerton, Mick Donnellan, Tom Leetch, Tom Molloy, Frank Walsh, Willie Smith, Denis Egan. BACK FROM LEFT: Fr Hughes, Leonard McGrath, Frank Benson, Sonny Burke, Mick Brennan, Bartley Murray, Paddy Ganley, John Egan, Gilbey Jennings, Jack Deeley, Larry Raftery, Jack Fry, Tom McGrath, Jackie Brennan.

Bernie Forde's Solo or is the Sliotar *Glued to His Stick?*

Galway corner forward Bernie Forde careers away from his opponent Pat Fleury (Offaly) in the 1981 final won by Offaly, their first Senior Hurling title. Injury or no injury, you could not halt the courageous Ardrahan man.

Tommy Joe Gilmore Catches High Against Down 1971
Great to see the skill of fielding the high ball in Gaelic football so well demonstrated by Tommy Joe Gilmore, contesting the catch with Colm McAlarney of Down in the 1971 All-Ireland Senior Football semi-final won by Galway. Sean O'Neill (14) on the right.

The Swig of the Magic Bottle in 1985
P.J. Molloy gets a welcome drink from mentor Tom Lenihan during the 1985 Senior Hurling final against Offaly won by the latter. Just what was in the magic bottle? Or was the Athenry man just parched?

Galway's All-Ireland Minor Football Champions of 1970
FRONT FROM LEFT: John Tobin, Tom O'Connor, Peter Silke, Joe Corcoran (captain), P.J. Burke, Joe Lardner, Maurice Burke. BACK FROM LEFT: Michael Rooney, Alfie Marren, Michael Meehan, Seán Higgins, Stephen Cloonan, Michael Geraghty, Iomar Barrett, John Kemple. Galway beat Kerry in a replay to win the title.

Galway's Big Three in 1987
Cyril Farrell's contribution to the success story of Galway hurling in the 1970s, 1980s and 1990s cannot be overstated. Here he is receiving a *Galway Advertiser* Award in 1987 with fellow selector Bernie O'Connor (former star) and dedicated official Phelim Murphy.

Two Dedicated Galway Football Officials Watching Galway Train in 1956.
It was a rainy night in Tuam Stadium in 1956 when this photograph of Galway's dedicated Football Board officials John Dunne (Secretary) and Fr Paddy Mahon (Chairman) was taken. They attended every training session in Tuam for years and years.

Galway All-Ireland Senior Hurling Champions 1923
FRONT FROM LEFT: Leonard McGrath, Ignatius Harney. SECOND ROW FROM LEFT: Andy Kelly, Jim Morris, Mick Kenny, Martin King, Tom Fleming. THIRD ROW FROM LEFT: Jack Berry, Paddy Hurney, Berney Gibbs, Mick Dervan, Dick Morrissey, 'Staff' Garvey, Jim Power. BACK FROM LEFT: unidentified, Fr Larkin, Tom Kenny. INSET FROM LEFT: N. Gilmartin, Mick Gill, Junior Mahony.

Gort — Galway Senior Hurling Champions of 1983
FRONT FROM LEFT: John Crehan, Colie Rock, Sylvie Linnane, Josie Harte, Mattie Murphy, Joe Regan, Gerry Linnane. BACK FROM LEFT: Brian Brennan, Gerry Lally, John Nolan, John Commins, Patsy Hehir, Michael Cahill, Michael Brennan, Pearse Piggott. Gort, always a wonderful hurling area which produced such stars as Josie Gallagher and Tadhg Kelly, defeated Castlegar in the 1983 final by 2-12 to 3-6.

Killanin National School Honours Three Past-pupils 2001
Killanin National School is situated half way between Moycullen and Oughterard. In November 2001 it honoured its three past pupils who had helped Galway to win the 2001 All-Ireland Senior Football Championship. The present pupils admire, from left: Gary Fahey (captain), former teacher Séamus Ó Cualáin, Richie Fahey, Kevin Walsh, Seán Bán Breathnach and the present Vice Principal Helen O'Connor.

The Castlegar team which won the County Cup (Galway Senior Hurling Championship) 1979 by defeating Kinvara at Duggan Park, Ballinasloe. FRONT FROM LEFT: Gerry Glynn, John Coady, Jimmy Francis, Michael Connolly (captain) Michael Glynn, Pádhraic Connolly, Gerry Connolly. BACK FROM LEFT: Pakie Connor, John Connolly, Joe Connolly, Tom Murphy, Séamus Fahy, Tommy Grogan, Liam Mulryan, Ted Murphy. This identical fifteen went on to win the All-Ireland semi-final against Blackrock (Cork) and Ballycastle McQuillans (Antrim) in 1980. This was the first team from the West to win an All-Ireland Senior club title.

Action Shot From 1984 Connacht Final
It was a scorching hot day in Pearse Stadium, Salthill, on the day Galway beat Mayo in an exciting Connacht final before a capacity attendance. Here Galway's Brian O'Donnell breaks ahead of Mayo's John Maughan to gather the ball. John Maughan later became a high-profile manager with Clare, Mayo and Fermanagh.

Rival Captains Share a Joke Before 1981 Senior Hurling Final.
It has always been the custom for rival captains to shake hands before tossing for choice of end before games. Here Seán Silke (Galway captain) and Pádhraic Horan (Offaly captain) share a joke before the toss of the coin in front of a packed Croke Park.

Galway All-Ireland Under-21 Football Champions 1972
Galway's first and only Under-21 Football title. FRONT FROM LEFT: Pat Burke, Barney Costelloe, Mick Geraghty, Joe Waldron (captain) Joe Lardner, Seán Stephens, Maurice Burke. BACK FROM LEFT: P.J. Burke, Michael Walsh, John Dillon, Martin Noonan, Frank Rushe, Tom Naughton, John Tobin, Michael Rooney. Galway defeated Kerry in the final by 2-6 to 0-7.

Team Manager and Player in the 1980s

Cyril Farrell has been Galway's most successful team-manager ever at College, Minor, Under-21 and Senior level. Here he chats with star forward Noel Lane while training for an important game in the 1980s. Noel himself was to follow the managerial route for Galway later.

Fr Griffin Road Vocational School Under-14 Football
I trained many teams to success over the years. This was the first one. We won the Galway City Schools Football Championship of 1962. FRONT FROM LEFT: Anthony Concannon, John Walsh, Pat O'Sullivan, Peter D'Arcy, Jimmy Brophy, Michael Faherty, Tommy Murphy. BACK FROM LEFT: Brian Cassidy, Colm O'Connor, Ronnie O'Connor, Paddy Flaherty, Brendan Casey, Eugene Flaherty, T.J. McDonagh, John O'Connor, J. Mahon. Those were the days.

Galway's First Ever Camogie Title (Junior) in 1972
Galway won its first-ever camogie title in 1972, defeating Wexford in the final by 3-6 to 2-1. Here Nono McHugh (captain) lifts the cup aloft with, from left: Margaret Killeen, Sheila Crowe and Grace Divilly on right.

Pancake Ward of Ballinasloe — Galway Mascot in the 1960s and 1970s

This photograph of well-known Ballinasloe character 'Pancake' Ward appeared in the official Connacht Final programme alongside Mayo's self-appointed mascot Paddy 'Blewitt' Greham in 1973. They used to march beside the respective captains. 'Pancake' never missed a Connacht final from the 1930s on to the 1960s and was a former Connacht flyweight boxing champion (1938–1940).

Iggy Clarke Limbers Up in 1980

When Galway reached and won the All-Ireland 1980 Senior Hurling final they had to field without one of their top stars, Iggy Clarke, who was injured. Here is Iggy limbering up prior to one of the Milk Superstar events of that time. Iggy is one of the greatest half-backs Galway ever had.

Galway's Senior Football Team of 1962 — Defeated Connacht Finalists

FRONT FROM LEFT: Pat Donnellan, Séamus Leydon, Brian Geraghty, Bosco McDermott, John Donnellan, Cyril Dunne, Enda Colleran. BACK FROM LEFT: Seán Purcell, Tom Magee, Mick Garrett, Brendan Glynn, Mattie McDonagh, Seán Meade, Frank Evers, Martin Newell. This was the day of the broken crossbar incident. Roscommon beat Galway in a thriller by 3-7 to 2-9.

St Jarlath's College, Tuam, Hogan Cup Champions 1977–78
FRONT FROM LEFT: Francis Stockwell, Jarlath Brennan, Gerry Murphy, Martin Joyce (captain), Pádhraic 'Oxy' Moran, Tomás Tierney, Séamus Cronin. BACK FROM LEFT: Aengus Murphy (RIP), Larry Heavey, Jimmy Lyons, Seán McGing, Liam Lyons, Seán McCormack, Robert Birmingham, Kieran O'Malley. The Connacht College Senior (A) Football Cup is now called the Aengus Murphy Cup to commemorate the Army Officer who was tragically killed on United Nations duty in the Lebanon.

Anthony Cunningham Raises Irish Press Cup (All-Ireland Minor Hurling) Aloft in 1983

Anthony Cunningham raises the *Irish Press* Cup aloft after being presented with it by Most Rev Dr Morris, Patron of the GAA. It was Galway's first-ever All-Ireland Minor triumph and his joyous colleagues celebrated too. They are, from left: Seán Treacy, Pat Higgins, Declan Jennings and Tom Maloney. Galway beat Dublin in the Final.

Galway's Under-21 All-Ireland Hurling Champions 1986

FRONT FROM LEFT: Aodh Davoren, Michael Flaherty, Pat Higgins, Gerry McInerney, Anthony Cunningham (captain), Tom Monaghan, P. Nolan. BACK FROM LEFT: Patrick Dervan, Michael Helebert, Joe Cooney, John Commins, Michael Connolly, Declan Jennings, Martin Kelly, Pat Malone. Galway beat Wexford in the final by 1-14 to 2-5.

They Could March in 1971 Too

The Galway team, beaten by Offaly in the 1971 final, march in great order before the game. Liam Sammon (captain) is followed by P.J. Smyth, Brendan Colleran, Jack Cosgrove, Noel Colleran, Liam O'Neill, Tommy Joe Gilmore, Coleen McDonagh, Billy Joyce.

Jimmy Cooney v Billy Fitzpatrick 1982 All-Ireland semi-final

This wonderful action shot from the 1982 All-Ireland Senior Hurling semi-final won by Kilkenny shows Jimmy Cooney, one of a great family of hurlers from Bullaun, racing away from Billy Fitzpatrick to clear to safety.

Action from Connacht Senior Football Final of 1965

An action shot from the Connacht Senior Football Final of 1965 in Tuam Stadium when Galway defeated Sligo by 1-12 to 2-6. Here Christy Tyrrell and Mattie McDonagh (number 11) watch as a Galway point sails over. Sligo wore white with blue trim for the first and only time that day.

Connacht (All Galway) Railway Cup Champions of 1987

FRONT FROM LEFT: Joe Cooney, Michael 'Hopper' McGrath, Sylvie Linnane, Conor Hayes (captain), Pat Malone, Tom Monaghan, Eanna Ryan. BACK FROM LEFT: Steve Mahon, Anthony Cunningham, Pierce Piggott, John Commins, Ollie Kilkenny, Martin Naughton, Brendan Lynskey, Tony Kilkenny. This was the team which defeated Ulster in the semi-final at Ennis on 3 October and went on to beat Leinster in the final at the same venue a day later.

Action from 1983 Senior Football Final

Brian Talty with ball, with Val Daly to his right urging him on against Dublin in the 1983 All-Ireland Senior Football final (won by Dublin) as Brian Mullins comes in to challenge while Dublin half-back P.J. Buckley (number 7) keeps a close eye on his direct opponent Barry Brennan (number 10).

Oranmore Camogie Team — Winners of the 1966 County Galway Senior Championship

FRONT FROM LEFT: Bridie Sheridan, Kathleen McGrath, Mary O'Toole, Rosemary Divilly, Bridgie Flanagan (captain), Mary Cooley, Ronnie Heneghan. BACK FROM LEFT: Kay Quinn, Sheila Quinn, Kitty Burke, Joan Cosgrave, Nora O'Toole, Anna Furey, Kathleen O'Flaherty, Rita O'Flaherty.

All-Ireland Senior Football Champions 1998 — End of a Thirty-Two Year Drought
FRONT FROM LEFT: Seán de Paor, Michael Donnellan, Ray Silke (captain), Derek Savage, Martin MacNamara, Niall Finnegan, Tomás Mannion. BACK FROM LEFT: Pádhraic Joyce, Tomás Meehan, Shay Walsh, Ja Fallon, Kevin Walsh, Seán Ó Dómhnaill, Gary Fahey, John Divilly. Galway defeated Kildare in the final by 1-14 to 1-10.

Kiltormer — Galway Senior Hurling Champions 1982

FRONT FROM LEFT: Joe Rodgers, John Goode, Tony Kilkenny, Tony Furey, Seán Cormican (captain), Kieran Lynch, Gerry Coone. BACK FROM LEFT: Seán Kelly, Liam Larkin, Frank Larkin, Martin Staunton, Joe Hayes, Brendan Dervan, Aidan Staunton, Ollie Kilkenny. Kiltormer defeated Castlegar in the County final by 2-8 to 1-9 at Ballinasloe's Duggan Park to win their third Galway Senior Hurling title.

Gay Mitchell Clears in 1979
Gay Mitchell, the Galway goalkeeper, clears his lines against Roscommon in the Connacht final of 1979 at Dr Hyde Park as Mickey Freyne (Roscommon) attempts to block the clearance; in the background is Brendan Corbett. Roscommon were victorious then.

Groundsman at Loughrea for a Lifetime

It takes all kinds of voluntary work to make the GAA tick. This is a photograph of the late Paddy Robinson, a groundsman at St Brendan's Park, Loughrea, for much of his life. Paddy won a County Senior Hurling Championship medal in 1941. Here he is gathering the flags, one of his usual chores.

St Patrick's College, Tuam 1988–1989 or Tuam CBS as it Used to be Known

Tuam CBS — Connacht Senior Football League and Championship title-holders 1988–89, pictured with their mentors Joe Burke, John Tobin and Kevin Dwyer. FRONT FROM LEFT: Michael Nolan, Tommy Wilson, Alan Feerick (captain), Joe Burke, John Wilson, Tommy Costello, Ollie Hynes. CENTRE FROM LEFT: John Tobin, Brian Mulry, David Coen, Derek Bane, Kevin Carney, Ronan Barrett, Michael Donnellan, Richie Lydon, Kevin Dwyer. BACK FROM LEFT: Brendan Quirke, Terry Delaney, Alan Kelly (vice-captain), Bernard Byrne, Francis Murphy, Trevor Burke, Tomás Tierney, Noel Tyrrell.

Galway's Inter-County Vocational School Hurling Champions of 1992
FRONT FROM LEFT: Declan Walsh, Martin Shiels, Niall Linnane, Noel Finnerty, Shane Walsh (captain), Francis Forde, Tom Healy, Finbar Gantly, Owen Fergus, James Treacy. BACK FROM LEFT: Peter Kelly, Michael Ward, Nigel Shaughnessy, Liam Donoghue, Dermot Hillary, Oliver Kennelly, Matthew Conroy, Derek Long, Gerry Carney, James Ward, Michael Spellman, Alan Harney. Galway beat Kilkenny in the final by 3-13 to 0-10.

Athenry — All-Ireland Senior Club Camogie Champions 1977
FRONT FROM LEFT: Anne Duane, Noreen Treacy, Mary Daly, Madge Hobbins, Teresa Duane, Anne Morris. BACK FROM LEFT: Anne Delaney, Marian Freaney, Midge Poniard, Breda Coady, Gretta O'Brien, Olive Coady. Anne Morris won the 1977 Galway Sports Star for Camogie. In the final Athenry defeated Portglenone (Antrim) by 10-5 to 1-1.

A Famous Photo — the Goal That Never Came

Liam Sammon won't thank me for including this. It is from the drawn Connacht Final (Senior Football) of 1969 against Mayo in Pearse Stadium, Salthill. Towards the end of the game Galway were on top and in a sweeping move all Liam had to do was tap a ball into an empty net for glory. But he was travelling at speed and his left boot halted the ball, and in one second Mayo had it cleared.

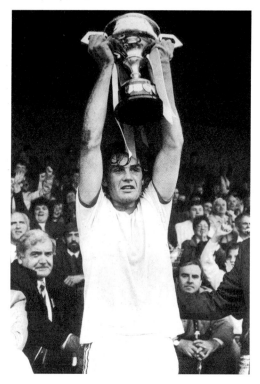

Pat Costelloe Raises John C. McHugh Cup (Galway Minor Football Championship) Aloft in 1988

Caherlistrane in Galway, home place of Dolores Keane the singer and her brother Seán, is a traditional Gaelic football stronghold. They have won few titles over the years but they soldier on. In 1988 the club won its first-ever Galway minor football crown. Here happy captain Pat Costelloe holds the cup aloft in victory at Tuam Stadium.

An Explosive Scene From an Explosive All-Ireland Semi-final (Hurling) against Tipperary in 1989
Galway players Brendan Lynskey and Joe Cooney share words with match referee John
Denton of Wexford, with Anthony Cunningham in the background. This was an explosive
game — the year of the 'Keady affair' when Tony Keady was not allowed to play for Galway
because of having played earlier in New York without permission.

Immortals All
A 2001 photograph of GAA immortals. It was a gathering in Galway to honour Frank
Heaney, Galway Junior All-Ireland captain in 1965 and former Irish amateur heavyweight
boxing champion. There to honour him were three Hall of Fame Gaelic footballers from the
past. FROM LEFT: Frank Heaney, Enda Colleran, Seán Purcell, Dr Pádhraic Carney of
Mayo. Frank Heaney who lived in New York died earlier this year. He is missed by his
many friends in Galway.

Man of the Match for Michael Coleman

Abbeyknockmoy won the Galway Senior Hurling Championship title for the first and only time in 1988. Here John McIntyre, Sports Editor of the *Connacht Tribune*, presents Abbeyknockmoy's star Michael Coleman with his Man of the Match Award immediately after the county final of that year.

Coleen McDonagh Clears

He was one of the tidiest half-backs ever to play for Galway. Here he is in the 1974 Connacht final against Roscommon in Pearse Stadium on a dreadfully wet July day, tidying up though challenged by Gerry Mannion on right, with Tony Regan (Roscommon) and Tom Naughton (Galway) on right. Galway won 2-14 to 0-8.

The Galway Delegation in London for Congress 1996 when Joe McDonagh was Elected President-elect of the GAA

FRONT FROM LEFT: Brendan Murphy, Michael Kelly, Joe McDonagh, Maitias Mac Donnchadha (Joe's Dad), Frank Burke (Chairman), Phelim Murphy. BACK FROM LEFT: Noel Lane, Miko Kelly, Michael Monaghan, Tom Callanan, Bernie O'Connor (Secretary), Pat Egan, Barney Winston, Tom O'Doherty, Norman Rochford. Joe became Galway's second ever GAA President.

The 1982 Galway Senior Football Team Which Won the Connacht Senior Football Title

FRONT FROM LEFT: Mattie Coleman, Richie Lee, Pat O'Neill, Gay McManus (captain), Steven Joyce, Pádhraic 'Oxy' Moran and Séamus McHugh. BACK FROM LEFT: Tomás Tierney, Barry Brennan, Pat Connolly, Pádhraic Coyne, Val Daly, Stephen Kinneavy, Brian Talty and Tom Naughton. Galway defeated Mayo in Tuam Stadium in a very one-sided final by 3-17 to 0-10, with Richie Lee scoring two classic goals.

The Long Lonely Walk of Defeat
Here Gerry McInerney in the Kilkenny jersey and Peter Finnerty (who earlier came on as a substitute during the final of 1992 against Kilkenny) take the long lonely walk to the shelter of the dressing-room after losing to Kilkenny on the score 2-17 to 1-15. The old Cusack Stand was still there then.

Corofin — County Senior Football Champions 1977
FRONT FROM LEFT: Gerry Hanly, Joe Stephens, Eugene McCarthy, Maurice Burke, Jim Sice, Ollie Burke, Frank Niland, Leo Higgins. BACK FROM LEFT: Martin Murphy, Frank Furey, Pádhraic Glynn, Pat Steede, Gerry Burke, Jimmy Duggan, Jimmy Bane. This was Corofin's third county Senior Football title and they beat Moycullen in the final by 1-9 to 0-3.

Army First Battalion, Renmore Galway Senior Football Champions 1951
FRONT FROM LEFT: Jim Brophy, Dick Quinn, Denis Heuston OC, Eddie Condon (captain), Fr Colm Whelan, Ned Cusack, Hugh McNamee. CENTRE FROM LEFT: Mick Downey, Pete Coyne, Jim Fives, Mick Meaney, Niall Sheridan, Paddy Kennedy, Tommy Moroney, Jack Kissane, Tadhg McCarthy (of 1934 fame). BACK FROM LEFT: Kevin Scally, Tom Coll, Billy O'Neill, Mick O'Toole, Sgt Major Tom McHugh, Peadar Mullins, Paddy Mee, Brendan Courteney, Colm Breslin. Army defeated Ballinasloe in the final by 1-4 to 1-3.

The Men Who Serve as Officials and Seldom Get the Glory
Fr Mattie Walsh served as Chairman of the Galway County Board from 1950 until 1958. Here the likeable priest from Clonfert Diocese (1911–1990) delivers one of his addresses at Annual Convention alongside Jack Whelan, the County Secretary from Killimor who served in that capacity for a much longer period and gave great service to the GAA in Galway.

Fr Griffins — Galway Senior Football Champions of 1967
FRONT FROM LEFT: Pat McSharry, Gerry O'Mahony, Bernie Power, Coleen McDonagh, Jim McMahon (captain), Ray Niland, Johnny Geraghty. BACK FROM LEFT: T.J. McDonagh, Michael Donnelly, Eddie Geraghty, Ray Gilmore, Christy Cunningham, Liam Sammon, Denis O'Shea, Eddie Dunne. Fr Griffins defeated Milltown in the final by 1-6 to 0-6.

1987 — History Makers — eight-in-a-row
The Galway Vocational Schools Hurling team which captured the All-Ireland title for a record eighth time in succession when they beat Offaly at Thurles in the final. FRONT FROM LEFT: Michael Curtin, Tommy Morrissey, Brendan Uniacke (captain), Oliver Kennedy, Kenneth Kennedy, Michael Killilea, Brendan Flynn. BACK FROM LEFT: Pat Hardiman, Pat Costello, Éamon Dervan, Pat Forde, Alan Kenny, Richard Burke, Eugene Keville, Richard Haverty.

Presentation to Dunmore's Mr Football in 1980

When Bertie Coleman retired as Secretary of Dunmore MacHales in 1980 after 28 years in the position (1952–1980) he was made a suitable presentation as a tribute from all whom he helped along the way. Eileen and Tommy Keenan (then Chairman) made the presentations to Bertie (second from right) and his wife Mary, his loyal supporter during a lifetime of football.

'Hopper' Holds Cup Aloft in Glee

The year was 1989. Michael 'Hopper' McGrath of Sarsfields holds the county Senior Hurling Cup aloft after defeating Athenry in the county final. On his left is the late Tom Callinan, Chairman of the Hurling Board at the time and long-serving Michael Mulkerrins on his right.

Connacht Railway Cup (Football) Winners 1957.
FRONT FROM LEFT: Tom Dillon (Galway), Jack Mangan (Galway, captain), Packy McGarty (Leitrim), Nace O'Dowd (Sligo), Mick Christie (Sligo), Frank Stockwell (Galway), Jack Mahon (Galway). BACK FROM LEFT: Frank Evers (Galway), John Nallen (Mayo), Joe Young (Galway), Willie Casey (Mayo), Ned Moriarity (Mayo), Noel Blessing (Leitrim), Gerry O'Malley (Roscommon), Seán Purcell (Galway). Connacht beat Munster in the final. Notice the huge crowd present.

Galway National Hurling League Champions 1987. Photographed in Thurles 3/5/87
FRONT FROM LEFT: Joe Cooney, Michael McGrath, Sylvie Linnane, Peter Murphy, Tony Kilkenny, Éanna Ryan, Ollie Kilkenny. BACK FROM LEFT: Steve Mahon, Michael Coleman, Tony Keady, Conor Hayes (captain), Pierce Piggott, Anthony Cunningham, Brendan Lynskey, Martin Naughton. Galway defeated Clare in the final by 3-12 to 3-10.

St Caillin's GAA Club, Ballyconneely. Newly Formed in 1956/57
Junior Football Championship West Board Galway. FRONT FROM LEFT: Michael Ferron,
Josie Conroy, Stephen Flaherty, Mikie Ryan, Martin Conneely, John Folan, John King.
BACK FROM LEFT: Martin O'Neill, John A. Joyce, Michael Kelly, Páid Kennelly, Francis
O'Malley, Patsy King, Jackie King, John Ward. This photo was taken in 1957. St Caillin's
do not field a team today.

Presentation Athenry Connacht Colleges S.H. Champions of 1969
FRONT FROM LEFT: Seán Hynes, Kevin Healy, Packie Flannery and Kieran Barrett.
CENTRE FROM LEFT: Gerry Cloonan, Luke Glynn, Frank Burke, Sr Brid Brennan, Mixie
Donoghue, Mickey Farrell, Fr Martin O'Grady. BACK FROM LEFT: Gerry Holland, Steve
Cloonan, Michael Poniard, Pat Kilkelly, Richie Donoghue, Mattie Lane, Gerry Corley,
Johnny Gannon, Michael Collins.

Action from Connacht Senior Football Final of 1984
Here Joe Kelly of Tuam clears the ball as big Tom Byrne (Mayo) comes in to challenge.
Kevin McStay is lying prostrate at the left while Séamus McHugh backs up Kelly. On the
extreme right is Henry Gavin of Castlebar. Played on a beautiful summer day; notice the
shirt-sleeved attendance in Pearse Stadium, Salthill.

Galway's All-Ireland Winning Minor Team of 1992
FRONT FROM LEFT: Declan Walsh, Michael Lynskey, Nigel Shaughnessy, Peter Kelly,
Conor O'Donovan (captain), Tom Healy, Michael Donoghue, Francis Forde, Dara Coen.
BACK FROM LEFT: Seán Corcoran, Colm O'Doherty, Michael Spellman, Liam Donoghue,
Cathal Moore, Shane Walsh, Kevin Donoghue. Galway defeated Waterford in the All-
Ireland final by 1-13 to 2-4.

I Lár na Páirce — Two Great Friends from Connemara

Kevin Walsh and Seán Ó Domhnaill in happy mood after defeating Derry in the All-Ireland semi-final of 2000; so happy that they swapped jerseys with their Derry opponents at the end of a close game.

1974 Senior Football Pre-Final Parade Galway v Dublin

The team is led by captain Gay Mitchell followed by Joe Waldron, then Brendan Colleran, Liam O'Neill (hand on head), T.J. Gilmore, Billy Joyce, Michael Rooney (hand on head), Tom Naughton, Jimmy Duggan, Pat Sands, Coleen McDonagh, Liam Sammon and John Tobin. Won that day by 0-14 to 1-6.

Gerry McInerney Receives Monthly GAA Award From National Irish Bank in the 1990s
A feature of the GAA scene for the past few decades has been the monthly Personality Award to GAA stars. First sponsored by B & I and at the moment by Vodafone. Here Gerry McInerney of Kinvara accepts a monthly award from National Irish Bank in the 1990s.

Joy After the Rain in Castlebar in 1992
This photograph was taken in the Galway dressing room in Castlebar in 1992 after Galway had beaten Mayo in the Connacht Under-21 final by 1-10 to 0-12. A huge downpour in an electrical storm almost halted the game, which was a close one. Tyrone subsequently beat Galway in the final. Here team captain Brian Forde and manager Bosco McDermott share their joy.

Brendan Lynskey in Action Against Tipperary National Hurling League 1998

Here in Duggan Park, Ballinasloe, before a packed attendance in an ordinary National Hurling League game in 1988, Brendan Lynskey, followed by Tipperary's Conor O'Donovan, fights for the ball with Tipperary sharpshooter Michael Cleary.

Turloughmore's First of a Record Six-in-a-row County Senior Hurling Championship Titles 1961–1966

Team of 1961. FRONT FROM LEFT: Jackie Gill, Alfie Galvin, Bobby Madden, Jimmy Egan, Michael Cullinane, Mickey Cullinane. BACK FROM LEFT: Michael Long, Frank Fahy, Paddy Delaney, Paddy Caulfield, Pakie Burke, Johnny Burke, Séamus Murphy, Frank Forde, P.J. Qualter.

Bishop Éamonn Greets Jimmy Duggan before 1978 Connacht Senior Football Final in Galway
The occasion was the Connacht Senior Football final in Pearse Stadium Salthill in 1978.
Here Bishop Éamonn Casey greets Galway captain Jimmy Duggan before the game,
watched by referee P.J. McGrath (Mayo) and Connacht Council Chairman Pádhraic Hunt
(Sligo). Roscommon won the game that day by 2-7 to 0-9.

Brendan Hynes Captains Galway to Success in the 1964 Senior Hurling Championship

Brendan Hynes, from Gurteen, with the Patrick J. Grimes Cup after leading the Galway hurling team in New York in the 1964 championship in that city. Prior to this Galway had won the New York Senior Hurling Championship title five times. This photo was taken in Gaelic Park — the home of the Gaels in New York.

Galway Senior Football Championship Team of 1954
FRONT FROM LEFT: Jack Kissane, Mick Greaney, Jack Mahon, Jimmy Halliday, Tom McHugh, Seán Purcell, Liam Mannion. BACK FROM LEFT: Jack Mangan, Iggy Hanniffy, Tom Dillon, Michael Hanley, Gerry Kirwan, Frank Evers, Mick Tallon, Billy O'Neill. This team against all the odds defeated National Football League champions Mayo in Tuam by 2-3 to 1-5. A huge shock then.

Féile na nGael in Galway 1981. Ardrahan Juveniles March Past

Féile na nGael, a festival of juvenile hurling, was founded by Séamus Ó Riain of Tipperary in the 1970s and continues to operate as a moveable feast of under-age hurling. It came to Galway in 1981 and here the Ardrahan team of that time march past the viewing platform in Salthill — a fantastic spectacle featuring 64 teams togged behind club banners of the respective clubs.

Séamus McHugh against Kerry in the National Football League 1979 in Pearse Stadium, Salthill
Séamus McHugh of Headford was a top class Galway defender in the late 1970s and early 1980s, winning no fewer than five Connacht Senior Football crowns, one National Football League medal as well as two All-Star Awards in 1981 and 1984. Here he bursts out to clear in 1979 past Ger Power of Kerry and M.J. Judge looking on.

The Presentation College Oranmore All-Ireland Senior Camogie Champions of 1972
FRONT FROM LEFT: Elizabeth Conneely, Margaret Burke, Noreen Connolly, Mandy Cosgrave, Teresa Carroll, Josie Kelly, Martine McDonagh, Marie Murphy, Mary Wynne, Geraldine Corcoran, Peggy Moran, Maura Armstrong, Marian Goode, Ann Finn, Sheila Cosgrave. The first team from Galway to win a Senior School's Camogie All-Ireland. They beat St Louis, Kilkeel in the final by 6-1 to 4-4.

Celebrating the Sam Maguire Cup in Sacre Coeur Hotel 1965
Though the celebrations then were nothing compared to now, this photograph, taken at a *Gaelic Weekly* Dinner in the Sacre Coeur Hotel in 1965, shows John Donnellan (captain in 1964) with Fr Paddy Mahon (Chairman Galway Football Board), Fr Jack Solan (Chairman Galway County Board) and Jimmy Ward (well-known Fr Griffins enthusiast and player).

Tuam Stars, Galway Senior Football Champions 1988

Any Galway pictorial book without a Tuam Stars team would not be right! These were the 1988 Galway Senior Football Champions. FRONT FROM LEFT: Brian Moran, Pat O'Neill, Tony Keating, John Purcell (captain), Gerry Bodkin, Willie Forkan, Murt Fallon. BACK FROM LEFT: Jimmy O'Dea (head down), Fabian Kelly, Séamus Fallon, Peter Warren, Ian Doyle, Pádhraic 'Oxy' Moran, Peter Keane, Conor O'Dea. Tuam defeated Corofin in the final by 1-8 to 0-5.

Fr Tom Burke's West Board Junior Hurling Champions 1960
FRONT FROM LEFT: Willie Concannon, Jimmy Flaherty, Tommy Small, Eddie Duggan, Paddy Ryan, Brud Flaherty, Donal Killeen, Pat Cullinane. MASCOT IN FRONT — Dermot Lernihan. BACK FROM LEFT: John Mernagh, Bernard Diviney, Peter Folan, Séamus Cox, Liam Cunningham, Jackie Forde, Manus Duggan, Pat Tom Corbett, Liam Wade, Michael Duignan. Fr Tom Burke's sadly are defunct for years but the memory lives on.

Fr Tom Burke's Club Social in Sacre Coeur Hotel 1961
1961 was a great year for Fr Tom Burke's, winning Under-16 and Junior West Board and County Cups. Here they are photographed celebrating at their Club Social. FROM LEFT: Donal Killeen, Mossie Power, Tom Diviney, Pat Walsh (captain, Under-14), Séamus Cox, Michael Duignan (captain, Junior), Pat McNulty, Stephen O'Brien, Mick Lernihan, Manus Duggan. The days of the trim haircuts.

Are You Here?

The huge crowd in the Gaelic Park New York Casino celebrate Galway's N.F.L. win over New York earlier that July day of 1965. The winning team and officials can be seen in the distance at the top table. We finish the book with this photograph, never published before.